# Eastern Gray Squirrels Invade European Habitats

T0025168

By Susan H. Gray

21st Century Junior Library

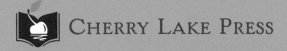

Published in the United States of America by Cherry Lake Publishing Group
Ann Arbor, Michigan
www.cherrylakepublishing.com

Reading Adviser: Beth Walker Gambro, MS, Ed., Reading Consultant, Yorkville, IL
Book Designer: Melinda Millward

Photo Credits: © When Photographed/iStock.com, cover; © Biotic/Shutterstock.com, 4;
© Giedriius/Shutterstock.com, 6; © Courtesy of the Library of Congress, LC-DIG-hec-42488, 8;
© Mircea Costina/Shutterstock.com, 10; © Nilanka Sampath/Shutterstock.com, 12; © Karel Bock/
iStock.com, 14; © beckariuz/iStock.com, 16; © Mark Medcalf/Shutterstock.com, 18; © RT-Images/
iStock.com, 20

**Cherry Lake Press** is an imprint of Cherry Lake Publishing Group.
Library of Congress Cataloging-in-Publication Data has been filed and is available at catalog.loc.gov

Cherry Lake Publishing Group would like to acknowledge the work of the Partnership for 21st
Century Learning, a Network of Battelle for Kids. Please visit http://www.battelleforkids.org/
networks/p21 for more information.

Printed in the United States of America
Corporate Graphics

# CONTENTS

Eastern gray squirrels are longer, thicker, and heavier than red squirrels.

# No Treats Today!

An Eastern gray squirrel sat on the ledge of a feeder. She could see all sorts of nuts and seeds inside. On the other side of the feeder, a red squirrel was stuffing himself. She sat and watched until he finished and scurried away. Then, she hopped over to his feeding station. Clank! The opening snapped shut. No goodies for her!

Eastern gray squirrels are a different **species** from the red squirrels.

This special feeder was built to **benefit** the birds and the **Eurasian** red squirrels.

The feeder was rigged. It responded to the gray squirrel's weight. As soon as the heavier squirrel hopped on, small doors to the food closed. The Eastern grays would have to feed elsewhere.

# Ask Questions!

Do squirrels live in your neighborhood? If they do, what are they eating?

While they may be cute, squirrels are wild animals
and do not make very good pets.

# Eastern Gray Squirrels Arrive

In the late 1800s, Eastern gray squirrels showed up in Italy and England's forests. These squirrels were **imported** as pets. But then, owners set them free.

## Make a Guess!

People sometimes keep wild animals as pets. Squirrels are very small pets. What could go wrong with keeping a pet squirrel?

Eastern gray squirrels can store more fat in their bodies.
They can withstand winter better than red squirrels.

Eastern gray squirrels and Eurasian red squirrels **compete**. The bigger gray squirrels eat more food. They feed on the ground and in the trees. The smaller reds usually stay up in the trees where they feel safe. Grays also carry a **virus**. The virus doesn't seem to bother them. But red squirrels can catch it and become very sick.

Both squirrels strip bark from trees. No one is sure why they do this. Perhaps they eat the moist, tender wood beneath. But the grays are champions at bark stripping. They can actually kill trees and ruin entire forests.

Female gray squirrels can have litters twice
a year. Litters can include two to four babies.

# Squirrels Making Trouble

Over time, people in England and Italy saw there was a problem. Eastern gray squirrels were rough on the trees. They were tough on the red squirrels.

Meanwhile, Eastern grays kept moving into new areas. As their numbers increased, the reds' numbers decreased. Something had to be done.

Eastern gray squirrels will make dens in holes of trees. These holes make good hiding spots!

Dealing with an **invasive** species always involves two early steps. First, people try to learn everything they can about the invader.

Second, they educate the public. Researchers talk to news reporters. Wildlife experts visit classrooms. Educators build websites filled with information. Meanwhile, scientists plan how to get the invaders under control.

# Think!

What else could people do to educate everyone about invasive species?

There are different traps available for catching
squirrels. The most common is the box trap.

So far, the English and Italians have taken these first steps. They put out special feeders. They have also tried hunting the Eastern gray squirrels. Some have tried trapping.

While these methods work, they are not working fast enough. Gray squirrels are still in England and Italy. They have also spread to Scotland and Ireland. But now, a new plan in Great Britain might solve the problem.

Red squirrels are able to outrun the pine marten.

# Hope for the Reds

The pine marten is a forest animal similar to a weasel. While red squirrels are able to escape the pine marten, gray squirrels cannot. The gray squirrels become **prey**.

## Look!

Look at a map of Italy. What other countries could easily become home to the Eastern gray squirrel?

Scientists are continuing to keep track of gray squirrel numbers.

Perhaps over time the pine marten will solve the gray squirrel problem. Pine marten populations are starting to grow. The marten is not an invasive species. It has always lived in Britain's forests. Red squirrels have always lived there too.

For the next few years, scientists will watch what happens. With luck, the Eastern gray squirrel numbers will shrink. And the little red squirrels will again **thrive**.

# GLOSSARY

**benefit** (BEN-uh-fit) to help in some way

**compete** (kum-PEET) try to outdo another

**Eurasian** (yer-AY-zhun) dealing with the landmass that includes Europe and Asia

**imported** (im-PORT-ihd) brought in from another place

**invasive** (in-VAY-sihv) not native, but entering by force or by accident and spreading quickly

**prey** (PRAY) animals that are hunted and eaten by other animals

**species** (SPEE-sheez) a particular kind of plant or animal

**thrive** (THRIVE) to do well and be successful

**virus** (VY-ruhss) a very small germ that can cause illness

# FIND OUT MORE

## BOOKS

Chung, Liz. *Controlling Invasive Species*. New York, NY: Rosen Publishing, 2017.

Lake, G. G. *Gray Squirrels*. North Mankato, MN: Capstone Press, 2017.

Murray, Julie. *Squirrels*. Minneapolis, MN: ABDO Kids, 2016.

## WEBSITES

### Biokids—Eastern Grey Squirrel

http://www.biokids.umich.edu/critters/Sciurus_carolinensis
Find a lot of facts about the squirrel's behavior, feeding, and babies.

### National Geographic Kids—Eastern Gray Squirrel

https://kids.nationalgeographic.com/animals/mammals/facts/eastern-gray-squirrel
Check out the information here about how the squirrels communicate.

### Washington NatureMapping Program

http://naturemappingfoundation.org/natmap/facts/eastern_gray_squirrel_k6.html
Learn about the Eastern gray squirrel's invasion of Washington state.

# INDEX

## ABOUT THE AUTHOR

Susan H. Gray has a master's degree in zoology. She has written more than 180 reference books for children and especially loves writing about animals. Susan lives in Cabot, Arkansas, with her husband, Michael, and many pets.